THE PASSPORT PAL PRESENTS
The Adventure to Snowy Forest

First Edition

copyright © 2008 Imagine It, Inc.

Story by Nicole Williams
Illustrated by Zoe Ranucci & Nicole Williams

All rights reserved. No part of this publication my be
reproduced or transmitted in any form or by any means,
electronic or mechanical, including photocopy, recording or
any information storage and retrieval system, without
permission in writing from the Author.

Edited by Imagine It, Inc.
Designed and Typeset by Zoe Ranucci

Requests for permission to make copies of any part of the
work should be mailed to the following address:

Imagine It, Inc.
9911 Rose Commons Drive
Suite E-159
Hunterville, NC 28078

ISBN: 978-0-9815385-1-8

Library of Congress Control Number
2008928738

Printed in the USA

THE PASSPORT PAL PRESENTS
The Adventure to Snowy Forest

by Nicole Williams

Illustrated by
Zoe Ranucci & Nicole Williams

To my sweet Ella, my baby, my muse, my heart.
Thank you for showing me what it feels like to be a kid again.

To my Don, my husband, my inspiration, my love.
Thank you for always believing in me.

NW

One warm and sunny day, four children met at their secret spot under an old oak tree. They knelt by the wooden box with the word "imagination" engraved upon it and opened it up with the excitement only a child could know. That familiar light shot out and forced them to close their eyes.

Their fingers and toes started to tingle. When the light faded, the children found themselves in their secret, magic world full of new and exciting adventures. Ella had transformed into a cat, Ethan into a turtle, Izzie into a pony, and Mila into a butterfly.

When they opened their passports, they found a map and the name of their destination. They were going to travel to Snowy Forest! After studying the map, it became clear to the friends what direction they needed to go.

They set off through the trees and suddenly heard a very noisy sound. They had reached Rapid River. Izzie and Ella found an old canoe on the side of the bank and carried it to the water's edge.

Mila found a very sturdy and comfortable leaf to carry her down the river. While the girls were getting situated on their boats, they noticed Ethan had climbed out on some rocks in the river. He turned to them, smiled ear-to-ear, yelled "canon ball" and dove into the fast-running water. Everyone knows that turtles love to swim!

The river moved fast and wild and almost bumped Mila off her leaf. The pals zoomed down the river so fast the trees on the side of the bank were a blur and the roar of the water as they sped downstream was deafening. Ella was holding on so tight to the side of the canoe that her claws were stuck in the wood. Izzie had both hooves wrapped around Ella's waist and was holding on with all her might. Ethan was enjoying the ride and at one point doing the back stroke!

When the river calmed, the pals knew they had reached the valley. Ethan was already waiting for them on the side of the bank and helped them out of their boats.

As the train approached, the ground started to rumble. The horn grew louder and louder, forcing them to cover their ears. The train screeched to a halt in front of them and engulfed them all in steam.

Ethan climbed up in the big engine, put on the engineer's cap, and prepared the train for departure. Mila, Izzie, and Ella boarded the caboose and sat in big, cozy chairs by the open windows. With a great blast of steam, the train started to move slowly toward the mountain.

As the train reached the steep slope, it was traveling so fast it shook violently and the wind whipped around the cabin. Up, up, up the train climbed and faster, faster, faster it went as it approached the top of the mountain. At the top, Ethan blew the horn several times to signal their arrival.

The train stopped with a jerk and the sound of steam whistled through the air. Mila fluttered out the window and fell to the ground as Izzie and Ella stumbled down the stairs and fell beside her. They were all laughing hysterically. Ethan climbed down from the engine and joined them in their laughter. What a ride!

When they finally composed themselves, the pals noticed a very long, steep set of stairs that seemed to climb up into the clouds. They ventured up. As they climbed, the ground started to shake under their feet.

When they finally reached the top, they noticed three massive volcanoes. They had reached Rockin' Volcanoes!

At the base of the volcanoes there were four musical instruments: a flute, a keyboard, a guitar and drums. Ethan picked up the guitar, Izzie sat at the drums, Ella stood behind the keyboard, and Mila picked up the flute.

The trail up the mountain was very steep and the temperature was dropping fast. As the four friends moved closer to the top, the snow started to fall and covered the ground around them.

When they finally reached the peak, they looked down on the most beautiful snow-covered forest they had ever seen. They had reached Snowy Forest! They soon noticed a small pond that had iced over and reflected the moon to illuminate the forest around them. The air was crisp and clean and the snow softly fluttered to the ground covering it like a white blanket. To their left was a sled, a snowboard, and an old pair of skates.

Izzie jumped in the sled and Mila quickly grabbed the ropes to help guide her toward the slippery slope. Ethan put the snowboard on and zoomed past Mila and Izzie. Ella picked up the ice skates and walked down the mountain to the frozen pond. The four friends continued to play until they were so tired they could barely stand up.

The End!